Pure Philosophy
Simplified for Youth

Pure Philosophy
Simplified for Youth

by
Muni Narayana Prasad

PRINTWORLD
Publishers of Indian Traditions

Cataloging in Publication Data — DK
[Courtesy: D.K. Agencies (P) Ltd. <docinfo@dkagencies.com>]

Narayana Prasad, *Muni*, 1938-
    Pure philosophy simplified for youth / by Swami Muni
Narayana Prasad.

        p. cm.
    ISBN 13: 9788124606032

    1. Philosophy, Modern. 2. Hindu philosophy. 3. Life. I.
Title.

DDC 190   22

© Author
First published in India, 2011
Second Impression, 2012
ISBN 13: 978-81-246-0603-2   **ISBN 10: 81-246-0603-X**

Published and printed by:
D.K. Printworld (P) Ltd.
Regd. Office: 'Vedaśrī', F-395, Sudarshan Park
(Metro Station: Ramesh Nagar)
New Delhi – 110 015-11
Phones: (011) 2545 3975; 2546 6019; *Fax:* (011) 2546 5926
E-mail: indology@dkprintworld.com
Website: www.dkprintworld.com

Preface

This small book was originally meant to be a textbook on "Philosophy," if included as a compulsory subject in all undergraduate studies in the Indian universities. The compelling need of the Government taking such a step is made clear in the "Introduction."

Now this is published with the hope that it will be of much help to the educated youth of India as well as all over the world, to give a shape to their lives with a proper understanding of life's meaning and how it can be lived meaningfully. I am sure this book will also help those who are fully grown-up and even elders, to guide themselves and their growing children. This is because having a proper understanding of the meaning and goal of life is a necessity that cuts across all barriers of religions and nations.

I always remember, with a whole hearted feeling, the interest Mrs. Brinda Erickson of Portland, U.S.A., showed to carefully read script of this book and finally to edit it taking much trouble. And many are my friends who enthusiastically inspired me to get this book published, and a few even offered financial help.

The interest shown by Messrs D.K. Printworld, New Delhi, to publish this simple-looking but serious book, is worth of appreciation.

I confess that the ideas and views presented in this book are not my own. They all are derived from the philosophy of

Narayana Guru, the scientific way in which my Guru, Nataraja Guru, re-presented it, and the simple way in which Guru Nitya Chaitanya Yati interpreted it. With prostrations at the sacred feet of all these *gurus*, I present this small book before the Truth-lovers of the world.

Sreenivasapuram   **Muni Narayana Prasad**
Varkala
1-6-2011

Contents

Introduction

THIS small book, *Pure Philosophy Simplified for Youth* was written to be a textbook for undergraduate studies in all universities, as a compulsory subject. Why it has to be a compulsory subject needs explanation.

The latest trend throughout the modern world is to groom the young generation to be money-making machines. Especially so after the advent of computerisation and globalisation of business. Such a channelising of life, in the normal course, begins as the youth enter the university level of their education. This really is the stage in life when proper value-based orientation with a well-conceived goal is to be made firmly rooted. Ironically, the younger generation who pursue professional careers, are unwittingly denied the opportunity to develop a proper view of the meaning of life, and also how to live that meaningful life. The omission of this opportunity at a *crucial* formative time leaves these newly educated graduates with no idea as to what they live for and show their skills for. Their yearning for earning more money becomes their priority one way or another. As a result, with no moral judgement, weak minds embody the potential to become criminals.

The authorities continue to try their best to universalise technical and professional education, because it creates more and more job opportunities. In the meanwhile, they fail to curb the criminal tendency which is groomed in the modern youth. This phenomenon is also creeping into the fabric of Indian society.

Take the case of a young person who takes to an MBA course in a university. What is basically taught in this highly skilled study is, how the money in the pocket of another could be skilfully brought to one's own pocket, or to the company one represents, with full consent and gladness of the other. A person who undergoes this professional training is never enlightened of the evilness hiding in such pursuits.

What is the remedy for this grave problem of global proportion? Bringing in a turnabout in the modern trend in education is not possible, and it is not what is needed either. I am confident that what is lacking in modern education could be infused into it.

Whatever one's livelihood, whether as doctor, engineer, lawyer, teacher, farmer or even ordinary labourer, all are to live meaningful human lives, and to do so they should have the awareness of the value and meaning of human life. They need an understanding of the nature of the world of which they are intrinsically a part. Then they need to know their real role in that world order. Therefore I feel the imminent necessity of the inclusion of a subject that deals with these, in all the undergraduate studies irrespective of the chosen course of study, whether humanities, science, professional, technical, commercial or any other. As is well known "Philosophy" is the only subject that covers all the above-said aspects. Therefore, I propose the inclusion of "Philosophy" as a compulsory subject for all undergraduates regardless of their chosen field of study.

Philosophy, as we know, is branched into various schools of thought and religious teachings. Which school of thought, or which religion, we should follow in order to implement such a scheme in the undergraduate studies of all the universities in a secular democratic republic like India, or in a world of various religions and ideologies?

Admittedly, the problem to be addressed is of a global dimension. Therefore, following any one particular philosopher would not solve our problem in a way acceptable to everyone everywhere. The entire human race, as we know, is divided into numerous religions. Which religion should we rely on for our purpose? Following one religion would naturally hurt the feelings of those who believe in others. Therefore, the best way would be not to follow any one particular religion. We really need a newly developed way of looking at our own lives as an intrinsic part of the total world and the total life-system. An impartial directive on how to live meaningfully as part of the whole is also needed. Such a philosophy that directly relates man with the cosmic life-system could be called "Pure Philosophy".

This small book is meant to be such a textbook on "Pure Philosophy Simplified for Youth". My sincere and earnest wish is that it would satisfy any youth anywhere in the world.

The first five chapters of the book deal with the basic problems of a fundamental nature, asked naturally by any human being, and how these questions are answered in the most natural way. The next three chapters concentrate on how to live a meaningful life in the most natural way. These chapters naturally deal with moral lessons. No direct moral injunctions are available in the world at present other than from the scriptures of religions. Therefore, the best moral lessons available from the most important world religions are joined together in these chapters.

How religion naturally becomes part of human life, and

what kind of prayer would be part of a natural religion are outlined in the last chapter.

I do not make the tall claim that the worldwide social vice in question would by completely wiped out by including this subject as compulsory in the curriculum of universities. An evil-less world, in fact, has never existed. But, definitely mitigating it at least to a certain extent can be expected.

I confess that the vision presented here is not my own; it is rather the extraction of honey from various flowers like perennial philosophers and world religions. And I obtained the overall guidance in doing it, from the vision of oneness of Narayana Guru, and the scientific representation of it by his wisdom-successor, his commentator and my own direct Guru, Nataraja Guru. I prostrate myself at their feet while presenting this book to the youth of the world.

1

Preliminaries

WE now enter a field of study that the entire humanity is always interested in. It deals with the meaning of our own life, the meaning of the existence of the world of which we are an integral part, and how we should live our lives in such a world. This branch of study is known as Philosophy.

What is Philosophy?

Now what is philosophy? The *Random House Dictionary* defines it as "the rational investigation of the truths and first principles of living, knowledge and conduct." What does the word "philosophy" etymologically mean? It really is a word compounded of two Greek words "phelein," to love and "sophia," wisdom. The word thus means "love of wisdom."

What is wisdom? The above-said dictionary again says, "knowledge of what is true or right, coupled with the right judgement as to action, sagacity, discernment, or insight." Again, "judgement" means "the forming of an opinion, estimate, notion or conclusion as from circumstances presented to the mind."

Originally the Greek word *sophia* had a much wider range of application than the modern English word "wisdom." Wherever intelligence can be exercised in practical affairs, in mechanical arts, in business, there is room for *sophia*.

Homer used it to refer to the skill of a carpenter. Moreover, modern English draws a sharp distinction between the search for wisdom and the attempt to satisfy intellectual curiosity. Briefly, then, "philosophia" etymologically connotes the love of exercising one's curiosity and intelligence rather than the love of wisdom as such.

This connotation of the word "philosophy" has more or less remained unchanged at least in the West. Generally speaking, each philosopher's attempt to satisfy his intellectual curiosity was always coloured by their own predilections. Thus the common goal of all of them has been to find a body of answers to all basic problems of life, formulated by reasoning. This has remained true irrespective of their leanings towards either logic or mysticism.

In the East

Different is the notion of philosophy in the East, especially in India. More than satisfying intellectual curiosity depending solely on reasoning, ensuring happiness in actual life, called *ānanda*, has always been the ultimate goal of all Eastern philosophers. In other words, philosophy for them is more of a value science.

Philosophy, in modern times, is thought of as the science of sciences, in the sense that it is the criticism and systematisation of all knowledge drawn from empirical sciences. (Ordinary sciences that have sense perception for their basis are called empirical sciences.) Also within the broad range of Philosophy come subjects such as metaphysics or ontology (enquiry into what is ultimately real), epistemology (science of knowledge), logic (science of reasoning), ethics (study of the moral value of human behaviour), and aesthetics (study of the principles relating to appreciation of art and beauty).

Here is yet another definition of philosophy: It is "thinking about thinking." As the science that systematises empirical sciences, the edifice of philosophy in the West was built upon the foundation of logical reasoning and association of ideas. (The interlinking or union between different ideas that happens in consciousness while thinking, is known as "association.") Both these originate from knowledge derived from sense perception or perceptual knowledge. But "thinking about thinking" can never have perceptual knowledge for its basis. The reason is, the "thinking" that is thought of in this case is not empirically perceivable. The philosophers who claim that all knowledge basically originates from sense perception are known as empiricists. Even they would admit that "thinking about thinking" has to be introspective. The empiricist's stand that all knowledge derives from sense perception is a notion. It is not arrived at either through sense perception or reasoning. It may first have flashed in the contemplative mind of the concerned thinker, and later could have confirmed it by reasoning. Such flashing experiences within the mind could be termed "intuitive visions." Such actually is the way all the scientific theories are found and established.

Admitting intuition as a valid means of knowledge is more natural with the Eastern Philosophy than with the Western. Of course, some thinkers of the West also give due respect to intuition. Therefore, defining philosophy as "thinking about thinking" could be treated as having a leaning towards the East, towards religion, rather than to philosophy proper as properly conceived of now in the West. This separation of philosophy and religion in the West had resulted as a reaction of the intelligent people towards the nightmarish inquisition. Thus an aversion towards religion and its dogmas became deep rooted in the culture of the

Modern Age, known as "The Age of Enlightenment," or "The Age of Reason." But such a division did not take place in the East. For this reason, philosophy in the East still continues to be rooted deeply in its religions. For example, philosophy in India is classified as Hindu Philosophy, Buddhist Philosophy, Jaina Philosophy and the like. This is one of the fundamental differences between philosophies of the East and the West.

The word equivalent to "philosophy" in India is *darśana*, meaning "vision." A vision of what? The vision of ourselves, the vision of our own life, the vision of nature as a whole, the vision of the Real. Each school of thought is also called a *darśana*, all aimed at the happiness of human life individually as well as collectively.

Wisdom

The word *darśana* presupposes three aspects, as does the word "thinking." These are *dṛk* (the perceiver, the knower, the thinker), *dṛśya* (the perceived, the known, what is thought of), and *darśana* (perception, knowledge or thinking). Both philosophy and science admit that one alone has to be the ultimate reality. The inner voice from within us also tells us so. If so, the knower, the known and knowledge cannot be three separate realities. They have to be three different forms in which one and the same reality expresses itself functionally. Then the knower realising himself or herself as that one reality in essential content, has to be the final goal of his or her philosophical search. It is equivalent to finding our own existence in that one reality. Each seeker (*dṛk*) thus has to realise, "I am that reality," just as a wave realises, "I am water." Attaining this transparent vision has been considered the essential content of wisdom in India. This wisdom, in Sanskrit, is known as *jñāna*.

Philosophy anywhere in the world attempts to answer two fundamental questions, namely, "Who am I?" and "From where and how did this world come into being?" Even my own existence as the knower (called "subject" in philosophy) is being felt by me as a mystery. The existence of the world I perceive (the "object") also is considered so. Even in modern science, at the sub-atomic level, what ultimately exists is found to be a mystery by quantum physics. So too is perceived by astro-physicists about the ever expanding universe and the outer space. Even when admitting "uncertainty" as a scientific "principle," modern science is reluctant to admit mystery into its precincts. Modern Western philosophy is no exception in this respect. But mystery is not an anathema to philosophy (darśana) proper of the East. Furthermore, the ultimate reality is always considered a great mystery by realised persons here. Such persons are known as jñānins.

The above-said two problems, closely viewed, are not really two. I, being a part of the whole, knowing myself fully and properly means, knowing me as an integral part of the whole world. That means, knowing myself involves knowing the world also. Likewise, the world is not an object external to me, because I am an integral part of it. Therefore, the world, for me, is not an object separate from me. Knowing the world as existing external to me, therefore, is not possible for me. Thus, knowing the origin of the world means, knowing my origin also. In other words, the above-said two problems are of such a nature that finding answer to one means finding answer to the other also. What we have recourse to in such an enquiry of ours here, will be our own commonsense and love for truth, rather than depending purely on "rational investigation" as the Random House Dictionary suggests.

2

Who Am I ?

LET each of us ask ourselves, "Who am I?"

Asked by someone, "Who are you?" my first response would naturally be, "I am Muni Narayana Prasad." But "Muni Narayana Prasad" is merely a name given me in order to identify me from others. Had I been given a different name, I would have been called by that name, even as I continue unchanged. That means, I really am not "Muni Narayana Prasad"; it simply is *my* name, not the real *me*. Then who am I?

I am now sitting on a chair and scribbling these words on a sheet of paper on the desk. Is it "I" who is seated on the chair, or is it my body? It really is my body. Then who am I? I am not this body, but I am the possessor of it. What is possessed cannot be the possessor; we know that my clothes are not myself. Is that possessor of the body the senses? No, because the senses are also *mine*, they are not *myself*. Is the mind that possessor of the body and senses? No, for the mind is also *mine*, not *me*. I really am the possessor even of the mind. Then who is that possessor? Here I am at a loss as to knowing myself; I feel as if I, in my effort to know myself, fell into a dark void. But within that dark emptiness shines an awareness of my own existence. That shining self-aware consciousness is what really "I" am. I, then, am that consciousness in essential content.

Suppose two people are sitting in a dark room; they do not see each other. One, feeling the presence of someone else there, asks the other, "Who are you sitting here?" The other man replies, "I," and he in return asks, "Who are you?" He also replies, "I." The two answering "I" means, a common "I" is present in both. This common "I" is not only in those two alone, but exists in all of us. This I-consciousness shines within all of us even when we are sitting in total darkness. When my eyes do not function, I remain in darkness as to the forms of visible objects. When my ears remain not functional, I happen to be in darkness with respect to sounds. So with the other three sense organs also. Even when I remain in total darkness as regards all the sense organs, I continue to be conscious of my being. This shining consciousness is the Real me, the Real possessor of the body, the senses, the mind and all such that are mine.

This I-consciousness is not in me alone. It is in you, it is in everyone, it is in every living being. Scientists also now admit that even a grain of sand, supposedly lifeless, has an element of consciousness in its being.* Then that grain of sand also could claim, "I am consciousness and I possess the sand-form as my body." In short, each individual entity is possessed by an individual consciousness. The universal existence should also have a universal consciousness that has this universe for its body. As we have already noticed, Reality has to be one. It is now found that that Reality in me is consciousness in essence. That means, consciousness has to be one alone; it cannot be many. The particular (individual) and universal consciousnesses then are not the real Reality, but are two different functional facets of one and the same Consciousness-Reality (let us write it with C and R capitals).

---

*   See *Seven Mysteries of Life* by Guy Murchie.

This Consciousness-Reality is not a consciousness about anything. It simply is the Consciousness or Mind-stuff that functionally unfolds itself as all the knowledges, all the emotions, all the mental functions, and even as everything perceivable and knowable. This last point will become clear later in our study.* This one all-underlying Consciousness as such never becomes understandable, because all understandings get formulated in that one Consciousness.

Our feeling still is that everyone of us has a different consciousness. How then can Consciousness be one?

Let us see. I am sitting in this room. I perceive directly everything within the room. All such things are known to me, and thus are within the range of my consciousness. What exists outside the room, I can imagine and perceive mentally; those are also thus within the range of my consciousness. While sitting here, I can think of what happens on the other side of the globe. Such events do not fall outside the bounds of my consciousness. I can also, sitting here, think of the inter-stellar space and even the outer space. That boundless space also is now within the ambit of my consciousness. Everything known to me, thought of by me, and imagined by me, is thus within the bounds of my consciousness, and the range of such things is boundless. Suppose something exists outside the bounds of my knowledge, like unknown objects or the unknowable Reality. Then, such things are *known* to me as unknowable or unknown. That is yet another knowledge. That means, such things are also not outside the range of my knowledge and thus, my consciousness. In short, infinite is the domain of consciousness. If that domain is imagined to be a circle, then its circumference is infinite in measure, and its centre supposedly is myself. In fact, one

---

* See Chapter 3.

dictionary definition of "infinity" is "a circle of which its circumference is nowhere and its centre is everywhere." How many infinities can there be? Only one. That means, even as appearing to be many, consciousness really is only one in number.

Then what about our feelings of separateness of consciousness? When imagined as a circle with infinity for its circumference, what happens to the centre of that circle? Something strange happens to the circle when its circumference grows to infinity — its centre can be anywhere, as was just seen in the dictionary definition of infinity quoted above. Therefore, even when the circle of consciousness remains one and unchanged, I think I am its centre; you think you are its centre; everyone thinks they are its centres. No one is wrong either. Only that all of them think and refer only to the centre of the circle, and forget the circumference. This forgetfulness on our part about our real oneness, is the fundamental ignorance common to all of us. Remove it, then we realise our real oneness. The shining sun appears to be dark to the closed eyes. Open them; then you perceive how bright the sun is. Likewise, open your inner eye that remains shut, then you realise the real oneness of Consciousness, the oneness of Reality, the oneness of "I" in everything.

3

Whence is This World ?

WHAT do we mean by "the world?" It, according to physicists, is constituted of matter. Matter alone, they believe, is the causal substance of everything. Mind, as they claim, simply is a side effect of certain chemical reactions that occur in the matter called the brain. The question that is not raised then is, "How is this material brain devised in such a way as to produce the non-material mind from it?"

Now what is matter? It is defined in classical Physics as that which occupies space and has mass. Occupying space and having mass are two qualities of matter. What then is the qualified that we call matter? Scientists must have set aside this question as a philosophical one, and therefore of no significance in science proper.

Matter ultimately, according to modern physics, is the non-material energy in essential content. That means, the non-material energy somehow assumes the material form of everything. If this mystery is admissible to science, why the non-material consciousness cannot be the causal substance of everything material? Either way, a mystery prevails in the creation of the world. Not only its creation, but the existence of the world also is a mystery.

As we are searching for reality, we mustn't be biased in our enquiry to the side of scientists who simply *believe* that matter alone is what basically exists. Our direct experience is that we perceive both physical and mental phenomena in this world, and that both are of fleeting nature. Mind is a subtle phenomenon, and matter a gross one. Our search should be for the one reality causal to both.

That matter is the substance of which everything emerges, is not a scientifically proved fact; it simply is a belief of scientists. This belief has no more scientific validity than the belief that God created everything.

Many Indian words, like *loka*, *jagat* and *prapañca*, are popular to signify the world. The word *loka* means, "that which is looked at". *Jagat* literally means, "that which always changes", and *prapañca*, "that which is constituted of five." These five are space (*ākāśa*), air (*vāyu*), fire (*agni* or *tejas*), water (*ap*) and earth (*pṛthivī*), together called *pañca-bhūtas*. None of these world concepts excludes from its purview mind or matter.

Most of the religious people believe in the existence of a world hereafter, besides the present one. If such a world or worlds exist, they also are not to be excluded from what the term "world" signifies in our present enquiry.

The idea of a microcosm, where the enquiry for reality goes from subtler to subtler levels of existence prevails in science. So too is the realm of a macrocosm, where the study extends to the outer space. Both these worlds also are to be counted as coming within the purview of the world we are concerned with here.

The world, philosophically speaking, comprises a wide range of phenomena. At its one extreme could be seen the subtlest factor of our own individual existence, i.e., our mind and its functions. Gradually assuming grosser dimensions, we have our senses, then our own physical body, and as a continuation of it exists the endless cosmic system at the other extreme. All these levels of existence are all to be seen as covered by the world we think of here.

Whichever way we conceive the world, it should have a cause. Put otherwise, if such a world is an effect, it should have a cause.

Undoubtedly, all mental phenomena originate from consciousness, called "mind" in modern psychology. Then what about the material phenomena? Analysis, we know, is the method of enquiry most favoured in the modern age, to find out any causal reality. Let us resort to it here also.

Take any object, for example, a piece of cloth, that forms part of this world. Analysed, the cloth turns out to be yarns. Yarns, further analysed, appear to be cotton fibres in content. These fibres, in the next stage, are found to be constituted of basic elements. Such elements, according to modern science, come to around 120 in number in the world. But the more philosophically minded Indian thinkers of the past conceived such elements as five in number, called *pañca-bhūta*s we have already noticed.

Our enquiry into reality at the microcosmic level lands us in sub-atomic nano-particles, which scientifically has been proved to be uncertain as to its real nature. This theory is known as the "Uncertainty Principle". Paradoxically, modern science, which is in search of certainty, remains satisfied with the notion that the ultimate reality that constitutes the world is of uncertain nature. The latest findings of quantum physics would have us believe in the paradox that the ultimate unit of matter is at once a wave and a particle. Particles are separate and distinct from each other, whereas a wave is unitive and permits of no such divisions. All the sub-atomic particles are determined to be waves of energy. Energy admittedly is a force, not a perceptible entity, it merely is thinkable. The existence of something that is thinkable alone has to be in our thought, in our consciousness. In other words, it is consciousness that manifests itself as nano-particles of energy, as atoms, as molecules, as basic elements, as cotton fibres, as yarns, as cloth, and as the world.

Seen from the traditional Indian perspective, the five gross elements (*pañca-bhūtas*) that we encounter in the world, are not pure elements, but are compounds of all the five. For example, the gross element "earth" has in it a major portion of earth and lesser quantities of all the other four. So with all the five. The basic elements pure and simple do not exist as such anywhere. These are known as *tanmātras* (the things in themselves), and exist only as philosophical principles or categories (*tattvas*). The existence of a philosophical principle, no doubt, is in our knowledge or consciousness. That means, according to the ancient Indian view also, it is consciousness that becomes unfolded as the ideas of *tanmātras*, as gross elements (*sthūla-bhūtas*), as cotton fibres, as yarns, as the cloth, and as the world.

Thus the one causal reality that underlies the various phenomena that constitute the world, is found to be Consciousness.

Let us look at the problem from yet another angle.

We have the experience of perceiving the world. Do we perceive the world fully? No, we perceive directly only a minute part of the world, and the rest of the world remains always unperceived. This unperceived part also is considered part of the visible world only because of the possibility of perceiving it directly if we go near to them. This unperceived part in our imagination, in our mind, is added to the actually perceived part as its extension in order to give a full shape to the idea of the perceptual world. That means, excepting a very minute part, the perceptual world exists in our mind.

Then what about the minute part directly perceptible? Let us take an entity in it, for example, a brass oil lamp. It is placed before you. You know that it is made of brass. That means, the reality in the lamp is brass.

It is the brass substance that appears at present as the lamp. Here, brass is the reality and lamp is the appearance.

Let us now try to know the reality part of it. You know that it is brass, and you feel your perceiving it. Does brass as a substance have a form of its own, though it can assume any form like the present lamp? No. That means, the brass substance is formless. Is it possible to see something formless? No. Then do you directly perceive the brass substance? No. Does it mean that brass does not exist? No, with no brass existing, no lamp can be made. In short, brass as a substance is imperceptible, but does exist. Then where does it exist? Only in our knowledge, only in our consciousness. The real existence of the brass-reality, thus, is in our consciousness. So with the reality of the world also.

Then what about the appearance aspect, i.e., the lamp form?

You are now seeing the lamp before you. Suppose you have never seen a lamp before and you do not know what it is. Then, would you recognise this lamp as a lamp? No. Why? Because only something already cognised can be re-cognised, the reason why such a knowledge is called "recognising." The already cognised lamp exists in your mind alone. It is by projecting that lamp-idea in your mind on to the object present before you, that you recognise it as a lamp. In other words, it is the lamp in your mind that you perceive as existing before you.

Still it is undeniable that the lamp exists before you, and that you perceive it. What do you really perceive? Is it the form of the lamp, or the lamp itself? It is the lamp-form that is perceived. This form is *of the lamp*, not *the lamp* itself. You, thus, do not see the lamp, but only its form, one of its qualities or attributes. Likewise, you may see its glittering golden colour, feel its weight, and all such qualities. None of these qualities *is the lamp*, they are all *of the lamp*. Closely examined thus, you realise that you are not seeing the lamp directly, but only its numerous qualities. You are seeing the lamp, the qualified, simply as a mental perception, and its existence is in your mind alone. So is the case with the world. What you directly see and know are countless qualities of the world put together; the qualified world as such remains un-perceived. Then where does the world exist? Only in your mind, only in your consciousness. Or Consciousness itself becomes configurated as the apparent world.

Thus from the points of view of both reality and appearance we arrive at the conclusion that what ultimately exists is Consciousness alone, that Consciousness alone is the causal substance behind the appearance of all the mental and material phenomena, that Consciousness alone is the one metaphysical Reality. In other words, the appearance of the world emerges from and in the Consciousness-Reality.

This Consciousness is what religions generally call "God." Muslims call it "Allah," Christians call it the "Father in heaven," Hindus call it *Brahman* or *Ātman*. Buddhists prefer to call it *Dharma* in the sense that it supports (*dhṛ*) the entire cosmic system, including the phenomenon of life in it.

Without assuming the form of the world, this Consciousness-Reality does not exist, and without this Reality existing the world-appearance cannot emerge. To point out an ordinary example, gold cannot exist except in some form or another, and without gold existing, the apparent forms like ornaments cannot exist either. The two remaining inseparably one is to be intuitively perceived by us. And this intuitive perception alone makes us satisfied of having gained the answer to the question "From where did this world emerge?" The answer is, "The world-appearance is the ever-changing form assumed by the one Conscious-ness-Reality."

4

How and Why Does the World Emerge?

ALREADY seen is the reality that the one all-underlying substance is Consciousness in essential content. The one basic problem that has puzzled thinkers from the very beginning, is as to the creation of the world from that one Reality. Religions treat the problem as if the creation of the world happened as a historical event at a particular point of time. So the problem they deal with is, "How the world was created?"

Creation really takes place even now, and it is a beginningless and ongoing process. As we have seen earlier, the Reality cannot exist without appearing as the world, and the world cannot appear without Reality existing. Creation, therefore, has to take place as long as the Reality exists. Therefore, let us think, "How does the world emerge from the one Consciousness?" instead of, "How the world was created?"

First of all it is to be admitted that an element of mystery lurks in the problem — a mystery, as we have already seen, acceptable to scientists, philosophers and religious believers alike. For this reason, giving a fully convincing solution strictly adhering to reasoning alone, is not possible. But a plausible solution could be seen found by all.

Scientists do not agree with the claim that a mystery hides in the problem, for the simple reason that admitting mystery as a reality is considered unscientific by orthodox scientists. Whether admitted by them or not, our common-sense tells us of the inexplicability of the phenomenon of the non-matter energy assuming a gross material dimension.

Then, how should we understand the event of the one Consciousness-Reality assuming the form of the world?

The all-underlying Reality, as we directly experience it, is of the form of our own individual consciousness. This consciousness never remains functionless; even in our deep sleep it functions as unconsciously enjoying the sound sleep. The same should be true with the universal consciousness as well.

Something to function on its own means, it has within it an inherent creative urge. This urge, never inactive, exists in the universal Consciousness-Reality. And to be active means, many transformations take place within itself. This results in itself incessantly assuming various forms. Such self-assumed forms of the one Consciousness appear as the world. The range of this apparent world known to us is from the most subtle mind to the most gross physical matter. The best way we can explain this phenomenon is this: the subtle mental aspect of appearance is the actualization of the subtle wilful imagination (sūksma-sankalpanā), and the gross material appearance, the actualization of the gross wilful imagination (sthūla-sankalpanā) of one and the same Consciousness-Reality.

The mystery in such a creation is often compared by Indian seers to magic. All the enchanting illusory appearances shown by a magician, as we know, is nothing but his wilful imagination materialised. As a result of the same kind of mysterious materialization of the wilful imagination of the one Consciousness, Itself appears as the world. This renders the very Reality invisible to our view.

For example, on seeing a wave one forgets to see it as water. Even our knowing activity, it is to be remembered, is a wave-like functional facet of the one Causal Consciousness. It is not possible for such a knowing function to know the Reality causal to the very function. The knowing function itself becomes a sort of veil put over the Consciousness-Reality causal to the very function. The same is true with the world appearance also. For this reason, it is held, the appearance of the world becomes a veil put over the very same Reality. It is just like the wave-appearance becomes a hindrance to see the water-reality.

Such is the nature of the creative urge inherent in the Consciousness-Reality. Treating it as a magic-like phenomenon, it, in India, is often thought of as *māyā*. And in this context, the Consciousness-Reality is poetically likened to a magician (*māyāvin*). The word *māyā* literally means, "that which has no being." When religious believers explain this mysterious element, they assert that nothing is impossible with God.

When the Reality unfolds itself in some apparent form, it means, some action or *karma* takes place within itself. This *karma* or the creative urge that causes the emerging of specific apparent forms, results also in the Reality's appearance as the totality of nature, called *prakṛti* in India. The word *prakṛti* has in it the word *kṛti*, meaning "action." The word *prakṛti* thus literally means, "that which is properly (*pra*) engaged in activities (*kṛti*)." Every minute element of this *prakṛti* is also active because nature as a whole is always active. This action of *prakṛti* in each of us seems to us as our actions or *karmas*. The main reason for such a sense is the fact that we have the free will to do and not to do certain actions. We having such a free will is also simply part of *prakṛti* functioning. The actions we happen to do by exercising our free will really take place as part of the overall functional existence of *prakṛti*.

All our actions, even the voluntary ones, in this sense, are to be seen as forming part of nature's actions. None of our abilities to do anything, mental, verbal or physical, is our own making. Therefore, making use of such abilities is to be treated as part of nature's functioning, not as our own actions. Considering such actions (*karmas*) of individuals as *theirs* is a basic ignorance in us.

Birth and Death

Then what about the phenomena of birth and death seen in the world? The creative urge or *karma* inherent in the one Reality always finds expression. It results in the emergence of new forms of appearance which are always everywhere. This could be likened to the emerging of waves in the ocean. It happens as an active expression of the inherent creative urge in it. The Consciousness-Reality could also be compared to an ocean. The birth of a new individual, then, could be seen as a new wave appearing. It disappears into the very same ocean. This is what we call death. Seen from the ocean's point of view, nothing is born, and nothing dies either. What happens is that the ocean of Consciousness exists creatively. Before the birth of a wave, during its manifestation, and after its disappearance, what does really exist? It is the ocean alone that exists. Likewise, before the birth of an individual, as he or she lives, and after the event called death, what does really exist? It is the one Consciousness alone that exists. It has no birth, it has no death. A wave could realise, "I am but ocean." Likewise, an individual, when enlightened, may realise, "I am but that birthless and deathless Reality." This realisation is often referred to as attaining immortality (*amṛtatva*). In the Christian context, it is known as attaining "eternal life," and in Buddhist terminology it is known as *nirvāṇa*.

The Why of the World

One of the fundamental features of the function of consciousness is that it, one way or another, aims at actualising happiness. The most sublime of all happinesses is of self-expression, for example, the happiness felt by creative writers and artists, when they express themselves through the medium they are familiar with. This is true with the Consciousness-Reality as well. It is always in the process of actualising Its own happiness-content, through Its own creative self-expression in the form of the changeful world appearance. It could be compared to a small child playing with anything at its disposal. The child creates without attachment, and destroys without attachment, engaged in fluid repetition of play, delighted and absorbed. Why does it do so? Simply to bring out the creativity that hides within and to enjoy self-expression. The same is the case with each of us. Whatever we do is always aimed at our happiness of self-expression. Only the nature of the happiness varies, and sequel to it, the efforts made also vary. Likewise, on the universal scale, the one Reality also, in order to see Reality for Itself and all the potentials hiding within, expresses Itself in the form of the world and the phenomenon of life contained in it. This self-enjoyment of Reality and the world appearance go on endlessly.

The religiously-minded Indians imagine this as a sportive enjoyment (līlā-vinoda) of God. The philosophically-minded hold that the very same Consciousness-Reality is also Happiness (ānanda) in content. The proof of it is that we feel the contentment of having known what we ultimately aim at in life, only when we realise the Consciousness-content of that Reality. It is also the realisation that the meaning content of everything, even of our own being, is nothing but this one Consciousness. It is this realisation that makes our lives meaningful, and thus full of contentment.

5

Actions as Such

WE now know that an individual's existence is as part of the existence of the whole. Then it follows that actions (*karmas*) of individuals and of the total Nature are not two. Nature's actions go on uninterrupted, and their course and style are unpredictable. Such actions in themselves are neither good nor bad; they are just actions. Then the actions of a person who constantly experiences his or her total identity with Nature, also are neither good nor bad, neither meritorious nor sinful. Neither do such enlightened ones have the sense of being the doers of actions.

Good and bad, merit and sin, are all ideas formulated by human minds based on certain value notions. Their validity is only in respect of human behaviour, not at all relevant in respect of Nature's actions. A person who experiences one's own identity with Nature is the one who finds himself or herself as a fleeting manifest form of the ever existing one Reality. He normally would not have motivated desires of his own, apart from what spontaneously arises as part of Nature's unfoldment. He sees his existence and Nature's existence as one existence. In his case, his mind and Nature's mind are one mind, his desires and Nature's desires are identical. He moves around the world free of all desires, free of all motivated actions, free of all sins, free of all bondages. He is to be considered a liberated one. Sin and merit, we know, are relevant only with respect to motivated actions.

Actions performed with the understanding that individuals have no actions of their own, and that all actions are of Nature, are neither sinful nor meritorious. Based on this philosophical principle, let's suppose somebody kills someone and then claims, "It was done by Nature." Is it admissible?

No. The simple reason is that a person of such a vision of oneness can never think of doing such a brutal deed. He sees himself as one with Nature, which also means, he sees everything in Nature as one with himself; he sees that what is Real in him is also Real in other beings. Loving oneself is natural with every being. In the case of a person who embraces the vision of oneness, his love for himself becomes extended as his love for all beings, because he sees himself in every being, and every being in himself. Then how can he think of killing another being, or even despising it.

The problem stated above does not arise in the consciousness of a person who experiences oneness of all. But problems and arguments may arise in a person who does not have that experience. Our intention here is not to argue about it or to convince someone else, but to live with the vision of the oneness for ourselves.

Living a life that transcends sin and merit is possible only with the enlightened. The unenlightened also have to live a righteous life. How is it possible for them to do so ? In order to help them, the enlightened ones, in the light of what they know about life, have formulated clear directives regarding what to do in life and what to avoid doing in life. Such instructions are known in India as Dharma-Śāstras or Smṛtis. In general, such are known as moral codes. In the case of Buddhism and religions that are of non-Indian origin, such moral codes find place in the body of their main scriptures. Whichever the religious tradition to which such moral codes belong, they could well be considered instructions on *dharma* (righteousness).

What kind of actions, then, are free from sin and morally sound? Those actions of ours that agree with the oneness of individuals and the total Nature. These are morally perfect.

Everyone is in search of happiness in life; no one seeks sufferings. Therefore, those actions that ensure one's own happiness along with ensuring the happiness of others are to be counted as morally sound. The actions that ensure one's own existence and the existence of the total Nature and the beings in it are morally sound.

How are moral codes codified? In order to understand this clearly, we should know what the word *dharma* is. Though used as a Sanskrit equivalent to "religion," it really is derived from the verb-root *dhṛ* meaning "to support." The word *dharma* then literally means, "that which supports."

Already seen is how the all-underlying Reality is one Consciousness. The unfoldment of this Reality as the world, though mysterious, is not unsystematic. It has a perfect order of its own, though not fully familiar to the human mind. This system that supports the entire cosmos and the life in it, is the real *dharma*. We and our lives form part of this system. When our voluntary actions fully fall in line with this system, they could be counted as ethical, fully righteous or agreeable to *dharma*. When our actions are discordant with the all-supporting system of existence, our actions become unrighteous or adhārmic. Thus *dharma* and *karma* always go together.

The enlightened, for the benefit of the unenlightened, have codified such codes of conduct, teaching us straightaway what is righteous and what is unrighteous, what is *dharma* and what is *adharma*, from time to time. Such rules naturally vary from place to place and from time to time. This is because what is practised in certain circumstances would not be practised in others. Therefore, such codes of conduct need revision from time to time, and it is being done in all cultures.

When guiding our free will and deliberate actions, such codes of conduct are a necessity in our human lives. These codes of conduct guide our virtuous action towards a favourable outcome. By making use of our free will, we are capable of deciding what to do and not to do. Of course, following such codes of conduct won't be felt to be a necessity if you are an enlightened person.

Sense of responsibility is yet another natural phenomenon in us. It demands that we make use of our free will to keep the course of our lives fully in accordance with that of Nature. The reason is our responsibility towards ourselves means, our responsibility towards the whole Nature, because "I am" is what is Real in the whole Nature.

A truly happy life becomes actualised when our mind and actions are in accord with the whole of Nature. This is accomplished effectively when Nature's will and our free will are brought to a single line. We can never bring Nature's will towards our free will because Nature's functioning is not in our control. Therefore it is essential to raise our free will to the level of Nature's will. In doing so, we make the known free will of ours agree with the unknown will of Nature. When this is accomplished, our life will flow with the unknown Nature. If we look to the Enlightened Masters and study the codes of conduct formulated by them, then the joining of the two wills can be actualised with ease in our actual lives.

Such codes of conduct or *dharma*s, it is to be remembered, are not meant to be just understood, but are to be practised. This practice ensures happiness in our life. Such practices always have the support of the understanding of Truth (*satya*). That means, Truth is meant to be *understood*, and codes of conduct are to be *practised*. Hence the famous dictum in India, *satyam vada, dharmam cara* (Tell Truth and practise codes of conduct).

Let us examine some such instructions on *dharma* that are universally acclaimed, in the light of the understanding of the one Reality (*satya*).

6

Some Guidelines Towards
a Virtuous Life

ONE of the best sources available to guide your life along the best of all possible virtuous paths, is to become familiar with the lives of the great men of the world. The hallmark of all of them is their simple living and high thinking. These are the best ideals anyone can pursue in life. Such masters lived as they thought, and they thought in order to live accordingly, and also to be role models to others. One's thinking, one's words, one's deeds — all three becoming in full accordance with each other, is considered one of the best human virtues, all over the world. This virtue, in India, is known as *ārjava*, meaning, "straightforwardness." You will experience this quality remaining alive throughout the lives of great men, while totally dedicated to the noble cause they live for. Mahatma Gandhi, Rabindranatha Tagore, Sri Ramakrishna Paramahamsa, Sri Narayana Guru, Ramana Maharshi were some such men in the recent history of India. The lives and teachings of Buddha, Jesus Christ and Prophet Mohammad are also highly inspiring.

The teachings of the unknown *ṛṣis* of ancient India are highly enlightening and rich in respect to guidelines on virtues. The stories of the lives of most of them remain unknown to us, some mythological legends apart. Even such legends are highly morally inspiring.

Direct moral instructions abound in such Indian epics as the *Mahābhārata* and the *Rāmāyaṇa*. The latter portrays Śrī Rāma as the best of all virtuous men (*maryādā-puruṣottama*). In the *Mahābhārata* story, when Duryodhana seeks the blessings of his mother Gāndhārī just before he starts for the Mahābhārata War, her response was, "Where righteousness prevails there victory avails" (*yatra dharmo tatra vijayaḥ*). These words are repeated many times in the epic. The implied meaning is that these are words to be constantly recalled as we live.

Personal Efforts and Chance Elements

Another teaching of high moral import is given repeatedly in the *Mahābhārata* concerning the fruitfulness of human efforts. All the efforts you make in your life, though meticulously planned, may not yield the intended result. Why is it so? Your efforts and their fruiting have to take place in nature. Events in nature have an unforeseeable course of their own. Your efforts also have to bear fruit as part of nature's unpredictable unfoldment of events. This does not mean, you do not have to make any concerted effort in life. The ability to do so is already in you as part of nature itself. So you have to make use of it. But you should be alive to the fact that the fruiting of such efforts depends also on the chance elements natural with nature. These two — your efforts and chance elements — are concurrent in what makes the intended result appear. Of these two, human effort in Sanskrit is characterised as *pauruṣa* (that which is related to *puruṣa* or human), and the chance element is termed *daivam* (that which pertains to fate). Always keeping this reality in mind enables one to face all life situations with a sense of calmness and equanimity.

One of the distinguishing features that is noticed in the

lives of great men and women is simple living and high thinking. The more you become aware of your place and value in the boundless and the apparently eternal cosmic system, the more you find how insignificant and fleeting your personal existence is. This awareness makes you feel the necessity of having a humble and simple life. On the other hand, to the extent you boost up your personal ego, unmindful of the total nature and fellow beings, you become tempted to have a boastful, luxurious life with a tendency towards sensuality.

Money is often the alluring factor that makes one boastful and mislead one's life. Yearning to earn as much money as possible is a trend you see in almost every modern culture. The only reason behind this zest for money is the notion that you can buy anything if you have money. If nature produces nothing, then money has no value. When you are hungry, you cannot eat money. All that you eat comes from and is produced from nature. Therefore, the primary duty of ours is to produce from nature what we need for our existence. One thing that money can never buy in life is peace. The more money you accumulate, the more it makes you peace-less. There is a well-known moral adage in India, that reads as follows:

To earn wealth is painful;
To keep it secure after earning is also so;
Getting is painful; so too is spending;
What then is wealth ?
Only a receptacle of worries !

Too much money makes life luxurious. And many think luxury makes life happy. Only those who live a posh life know their worries. They find it impossible to sleep at night without keeping a loaded pistol under their pillows. A poor man, on the other hand, sleeps soundly with no worries.

Whom do we consider great? Those who are well aware

of the meaning of life, who have a transparent vision of what is ultimately real, who teach through their words and deeds, what they have realised. They really know their own place in this unimaginably expansive universe; they are alive to their insignificance as individuals forming part of this boundless cosmos. Therefore this wisdom makes them more and more humble.

The man ignorant of the nature of life, who nurtures the notion that it is money that measures the value of life, boosts up his ego much as he accumulates money. Finally, without inner peace, he leaves the world as well as all the money he had procured painfully.

Also to be known is the fact that money is not a product of nature; it simply is a convenient means of exchanging commodities, devised by man. If you are not cautious enough, this "means of exchange" has the potential to rob you of all peace in your life. Avoiding this tragedy requires you to have a discreet attitude towards money.

Then, don't we need money? Yes, we do. With no money at hand we cannot buy what we are essentially in need of for our existence; we cannot get educated; we cannot avail hospital treatments when we are sick. We do need money, but just enough for all such essential purposes and not more. We should only buy what we need using money; money should never be allowed to buy us. That means, we have to be capable of curbing our quest for wealth for its own sake.

Don't we have to possess wealth for the well-being of our children? Yes, we have to save money to ensure their upkeep, for their education and other necessities, until they are grown up capable of earning on their own. Accumulating wealth for an effortless life of children simply makes them idle and thus morally corrupt. Nature also endows them with all the abilities to work with their own hands and minds. Not letting them do so corrupts them. Therefore, accumulating wealth to ensure effortless existence of the next generation makes parents the enemies of their own children.

Human dignity is not enhanced by money and the luxurious life it buys. It is high thinking that enriches the life of man. Man, as we know, is defined as "the thinking animal." The only feature that separates human life from animal life, is man's thinking habit. The higher one's thoughts, the nobler life becomes. When high thinking is lacking, and when the priority is focused on a material, luxurious life, man remains an animal that has a refined life, but not a refined human life. The human nature in man becomes outstanding only when he resorts to high thinking, which is naturally reflected by his simple living.

We do need money to meet our daily needs. Such is the way the social aspect of human life developed through various stages of history. In one way, money does ensure our worldly happiness. The way we earn money should be such that it also ensures our inner happiness. That means, money ought to be earned by doing works that fully befit your inner nature. You will enjoy doing such works, and you will then feel, time runs very fast. Doing works unfit for your personal traits keeps you unhappy all through your work, and you will feel, time drags on. Therefore, before you choose a job, you have to carefully think of the nature of the work, you have to be fully aware of your inner propensities, and you have to weigh whether the job fits you. Such a fitting job in India is known as one's *svadharma*. And such means of earning livelihood has to be righteous as well. If you find that what makes you happy is some unrighteous job, it indicates the urgent need of correcting yourself.

Wealth, in modern times, is acquired through various means. There are three classifications of such means in India. One, the wealth earned through one's own efforts. This is considered the best of all wealths (*uttama-dhana*). The next, those inherited by us. This is counted as of the medium order (*madhyama-dhana*), and all else are of inferior status (*adhama-dhana*).

The best of all wealths, it should always be remembered, is the wealth of knowledge, and wisdom is the highest of all knowledges.

Conscience

One of the very forceful psychological factors as part of nature, that guides us in our actions is conscience. Even when nature takes its own course in us, conscience as part of it often forbids some of these actions. You should practise harmonising the outer flow of your actions with the conscience that forms part of your inner nature. This self-imposed effort to restrain your own external actions is known as *ātma-saṁyamana*.

How can you be happy in life, especially when dealing with others ? Be just, and you will be happy. Conscience always commands you to be just. What is justice? That love of order which creates order, we call goodness, and that order which preserves order we call justice. Justice and goodness are inseparable. To exist in accordance with nature is the best goodness and dignity. Preserving nature's order is the best of all justices.

It is only when we haggle with conscience that we have recourse to subtleties of arguments. Conscience, when not conditioned by relativistic social mores, never deceives us; she is the true guide of man. And this conscience is in us as a divine gift of nature; as a mysterious function of nature.

What is this conscience in essential content ? There is at the bottom of our hearts an innate principle of justice and virtue. This principle calls us from within, despite our maxims, to judge our own actions and the actions of others to be good or evil. It is this principle that we should call conscience.

What then is virtue? Virtue is love of order. Which order is it? Nature's order. How can it be respected by humans? The virtuous man orders his life with full regard to all men, to all creatures, and to all creation. The wicked one orders life for self alone, centring all things around himself. The other measures his radius and remains at the circumference. Thus his place depends on the common centre, the one Reality.

Self-Restraint

To be virtuous in life and to attune your life to the overall flow of nature require a constant watchfulness and self-restraint on your part. Seeking happiness is natural with all living beings; we human beings are no exception. With other living beings, it is achieved through some efforts that instinctively happen. It is not so with humans. Even above the instinctive level, they make use of their will, reasoning and skill, all controlled by conscience, in a very complex way to achieve this goal. Whatever be the nature of happiness we achieve thus, it has to well up from within our own being. The external objects, thought of as pleasure-giving, serve only as an instrument to rouse to action the happiness already within us. The external objects are so structured by nature that their charm kindles the happiness in our own being. The senses in us serve only as a medium between us and the objects.

We experience this more clearly in our eating. We feel hungry. This hunger is within and the substances that satisfy it exist outside. When eaten, it causes the happiness of satisfying the hunger. The hunger within and the substances without are so intrinsically related to the union of the two, which results in the actualisation of the happiness that was already dormant within. The same is true with the function of sense organs. Therefore, as your sense organs get into contact with pleasure-giving objects outside, instead of becoming infatuated and distracted by them, what you have to feel is the mysteriousness and glory of nature. Everything in this nature is so arranged that your contact with something outside arouses the happiness already within you. On perceiving this glory, your interest naturally turns to the happiness in you and the Reality in you, rather on the pleasure the objects supposedly give. The more you become interested in the happiness within you, the more you become withdrawn from the interest on pleasurable objects. This double-sided discipline — attuning yourself to the happiness within and to the glory of nature on the one side, and withdrawing the desire for seeking pleasures from outside on the other — forms the essential content of self-restraint.

The same kind of potential distractions is possible in the realm of the functions of your mind as well. Mind is some-how so devised by nature that its fanciful ideas, imaginations, ideals, aspirations and expectations of having pleasure may mislead you from your chosen path and goal. The stabilised notion that your happiness abides in your own being, can help you to withhold your own mind from its misguided notions.

The functions of your mind are also really to be seen as forming an integral part of the unfoldment of nature. Then you become capable of being a witness to the functional beingness of the one nature including the functions of your own mind. This perception could well be aided by your deliberate attempt to withhold your mind at once whenever it becomes distracted.

Such a self-restraint in the realms both of sense contacts and mental functions enables you to achieve a well-balanced state and thus a lasting happiness in life.

Another common human frailty is imitating others who are unworthy, and attempting to live or behave like them. The men really worthy of being imitated by ordinary people are the great ones we have already spoken of. They were men who have imitated none. On the other hand, they lived their own lives along the path of virtue chosen by them. What they aspired to attain was not the false vainglorious behaviour of others, but the glory of what was Real within themselves. Reading the autobiographies or biographies of such great souls would guide you in this regard. The best ideal, then, is to live your own life and to be happy with yourself.

Many think, their happiness depends on the recognition others give them, or the good company of others. Really we were born alone. Our death also will take place alone. The life in between also becomes meaningful when lived alone, i.e. by living one's own life even when being with others.

7

Some Direct Moral Instructions

ETHICAL thoughts are an attempt to formulate codes and
principles of moral behaviour, and this has always been a
necessary feature of human culture everywhere. Why is it so?

Man by nature has a divine gift of free will. That means,
he prefers to make free decisions which determine the course
of his life. Denying this free will renders human life
worthless. On the other hand, he has to live as part of the
world, in harmony with nature. He does not have much
control over the course of events in nature. Therefore, to
ensure his existence is harmonious with nature, he needs to
arrange his free choices so that they are in harmony with
nature. These choices need to be made regardful to the
interests of fellow human beings. The attempt to do so
resulted in the development of ethics as a branch of
philosophy. We will not go into a detailed study of the ethical
principles which we have already covered summarily.

Moral teachings abound in all religions, and all religions
have their own separate scriptures. Still much similarity exists
among all of these teachings in respect to moral codes. This
is because human aspirations and goals of life are one and
the same everywhere and always.

In India, the scriptures that teach how one should behave
in life, and how one should not, are known as Smṛtis,
meaning "that which is remembered and always to be

remembered," and those containing pure philosophical teachings, Śrutis (that which is heard). The separation of scriptures into these sets is not seen in such religions as Buddhism, Christianity, Islam, Judaism and the Far Eastern religions.

Of all religions of Indian origin, Buddhism contains some direct moral instructions of eternal value. Such teachings could generally be classified as prohibitions (niṣedhas) and injunctions (vidhis). The Buddhist prohibitions are known as pañca-śīlas (five noble habits). These are,

1. Do not steal.
2. Do not kill.
3. Do not have illegitimate sexual affairs.
4. Do not lie.
5. Do not drink.

These instructions of the nature of injunctions appear in Buddhism as part of its Four Noble Truths (ārya-satyas), the most basic of all Buddhist teachings. The Four Noble Truths are these:

1. *The Noble Truth of Suffering*: The fact that life is full of sufferings; birth is painful; decay causes sufferings; death causes suffering. Sorrow, lamentations, pain, grief and despair are all sufferings.

2. *The Noble Truth of the Origin of Sufferings*: That craving (āśā) is the cause of all sufferings.

3. *The Noble Truth of the Cessation of Suffering*: That complete extinction of craving, the rejection, dispelling, freeing, getting out of it, ensures the cessation of sufferings.

On having a desire (āśā), one strives to make it fruitful. Any failure in achieving it causes disappointment (nirāśā) which always is painful. In the event of having no desire at all, there is no room for any disappointment either.

4. *The Noble Truth of the Path*: That leads you to the end of sufferings.

The following of the Noble Eightfold Path (*aṣṭāṅga-mārga*) ensures the extinction of cravings.

These Eightfold Paths are :

1. Right Understanding (*samyag-dṛṣṭi*).

2. Right-mindedness (*samyak-saṅkalpa*).

3. Right Speech (*samyag-vāk*).

4. Right Action (*samyak-karma*).

5. Right Living (*samyag-ājīva*)

6. Right Effort (*samyag-vyāyāma*).

7. Right Attentiveness (*samyak-smṛti*).

8. Right Concentration (*samyak-samādhi*).

1. What is Right Understanding (*samyag-dṛṣṭi*)?

When you understand evil and the roots of evil, when you understand good and the roots of good, it is Right Understanding (*samyag-dṛṣṭi*).

What is evil?

(a) Killing is evil.

(b) Stealing is evil.

(c) Unlawful sexual relationship is evil.

(d) Lying is evil.

(e) Slandering is evil.

(f) Using harsh language is evil.

(g) Vain talk is evil.

(h) Covetousness is evil.

(i) Cruelty is evil.

(j) Wrong views are evil.

Greed, anger and delusion are the roots of evil.

Freedom from greed, freedom from anger and freedom from delusion are the roots of good.

When one understands suffering and the cause of suffering, when one understands the cessation of suffering and the Path that leads to the cessation of suffering, this is Right Understanding (*samyag-dṛṣṭi*), or when one sees that forms, feelings, perceptions, tendencies and consciousness are all transient, he then has Right Understanding.

2. What is Right-mindedness (*samyak-saṅkalpa*)?

(a) The thought free from sensuality.

(b) The thought free from ill-will.

(c) The thought free from cruelty.

These form Right-mindedness.

3. What is Right Speech (*samyag-vāk*)?

Overcome lying and abstain from telling falsehood, speak truth, be devoted to truth, and adhere to truth. Then you become worthy of confidence; no deceiver of men becomes so.

Overcome slandering and abstain from abuse. What a man of right speech hears here, he does not repeat it anywhere else, because recycling gossip creates dissension; what he has heard anywhere, he does not repeat here so as to cause dissension. Thus he brings together those that are at variance; establishes those that are united; and concord makes him glad.

Give up harsh language, abstain from hard language. Speak words that are free from rudeness, that are soothing to ears, loving, going to the heart, courteous, rejoicing many, elevating many.

Overcome vain talks, abstain from vain talks. He who speaks at the right time, speaks in accordance with facts, speaks to the point, his speech is of real value.

4. What is Right Action (*samyak-karma*)?

Give up killing; abstain from killing. Without stick or sword, but with compassion, full of sympathy, cherish kindness and pity for all living beings.

Give up stealing; abstain from stealing. Take only what is given you. Do not take away with thievish intent what another person possesses if not given you.

Give up unlawful sexual intercourse, abstain from unlawful sexual intercourse. Do not have intercourse with under-age girls under the protection of fathers, mothers, elders, brothers, sisters or relatives, nor with women married to others, nor with erotic dancing girls and prostitutes. These exemplify Right Action.

5. What is Right Living (*samyag-ājīva*)?

When you renounce a wrong way of living that you feel unfit to you, and get your livelihood by a right means that is befitting you, it is Right Living.

Five trades have to be avoided by one as an adherent to Right Living. These are, trading in arms, trading in living beings, trading in flesh, trading in intoxicating drinks, and trading in poison.

6. What is Right Effort (*samyag-vyāyāma*)?

There are four great efforts:

    (a) The effort to avoid.

    (b) The effort to overcome.

    (c) The effort to develop.

    (d) The effort to maintain.

The "effort to avoid" means, you beget in yourself the will not to permit evils (unwholesome things that have not yet arisen). Summoning all your strength, you struggle, you strive, and you incite your mind.

The "effort to overcome" means, you beget in yourself the will to overcome evil (unwholesome things that have not already arisen). Summoning all your strength, you struggle, you strive, and you incite your mind. You do not allow a thought of greed, anger, delusion that has already arisen to find foothold, you suppress it, you expel it, and you cause it to disppear.

The "effort to develop" means, you struggle and strive to summon your strength to let this habit grow in you, and you let thoughts of good take root in you.

The "effort to maintain" means, you struggle and strive to retain the good habits thus developed.

Suppose someone openly asserts, "I want to do what I like, and I will do what I like; nobody can stop me from doing so." Will not such actions clash with the actions of another who chooses to do something else on the same occasion? Will not many such actions go against the prevailing State laws and generally acknowledged value notions? Here we experience the value of the Right Efforts described above.

7. What is Right Attentiveness (*samyak-smṛti*)?

The only way that leads us mortals to the attainment of purity, to the overcoming of sorrow and lamentations, to the cessastion of suffering and grief, to the entering upon the right path and the realisation of the final goal of life, is the four fundamentals of Attentiveness:

(a) Live in Contemplation of the Body.

(b) Live in Contemplation of the Sensations.

(c) Live in Contemplation of the Mind.

(d) Live in Contemplation of the Internal Phenomena.

These are to be practised unwaveringly while being clearly conscious, with senses awake, and having overcome worldly desires and sorrows.

8. What is Right Concentration (*samyak-samādhi*)?

One-pointedness of mind is Right Concentration.

The Four Fundamentals of Attentiveness (see item 7 above) are the objects of *samādhi* or Concentration. That means, when your attention is totally on the existence and functions of your body, then you are in *samyak-samādhi*.

When your attention is concentrated totally on the sensations that occur in your being, then you are in *samyak-samādhi*.

When you are fully awake to the functions of your mind, then you are in *samyak-samādhi*.

When you concentrate your attention on the internal phenomena in you, then you are in *samyak-samādhi*.

The Four Great Efforts (see item 6 above) are the means of attaining this *samādhi*.

(The preceding analysis of Buddhist Ethics was culled from *The Wisdom of Buddhism*, edited by Christmas Humphrey, Rider and Company, London, 1970.)

Kindness of Life

Not to kill and to be kind to living beings are held as some of the highest human values by all great men as well as by all religions. This is especially true in Buddhism.

Do you like yourself to be killed and eaten? No. Also other beings do not want to be killed and eaten. The habit of not hurting is known as *ahiṁsā* in India.

Killing other beings and eating them defines you as a beast; not hurting other beings defines you as as a human.

In modern life, especially in big towns and cities, you do not have to kill in order to eat meat; you can buy meat from the market. It requires others to kill for you, in order for you to eat meat. Your eating meat thus makes others kill. Doing so is more sinful than you killing directly.

In principle, you killing another being means, you killing yourself, because the essential Substance in you and other beings is one and the same Consciousness. Thus, you are they, and they are you. How can you then kill another being and eat it mercilessly?

Eating meat makes you impure also. For example, taking part in funeral ceremonies, according to Indian customs, makes you impure; so you would have to dip yourself three times in water before entering your own house. Some close relatives of the deceased may have to carry the dead body to the burial ground or pyre. By doing so, they become more impure; hence they would have to dip themselves in water twelve times before going back home. Then what about the impurity caused by eating a dead body? Is it not dead bodies that the meat-eaters eat ? Or, do you like to make yourself the burial ground of dead-bodies ?

It could well be asked, "Is it possible to eat anything without hurting some other living entity? Is there not hurting in eating vegetables?" Yes, there is hurting in it. Here also it is your conscience rather than your reasoning that should help you make a decision. Is it the same way your feelings are hurt when you cut or pluck a vegetable that grow in your garden, and when you cut the throat of a rooster or hen that you raise in your own premises and feed with your own hands? Certainly not. Let your own conscience decide whether you should kill animals, birds and fish just to please your palate.

Admittedly the source of all food items is organic matter. If you are mindful of counting non-hurting as a high human value, then you will have to draw a line to mark the limit of your hurting for survival. Even among vegetables, as you find when closely observed, certain items involve no hurting at all; for example, certain roots like tapioca. Eating its roots in no way causes destruction to its next generation. Likewise, eating most of the fruits does not entail any hurting. All the fruits, in fact, are meant by nature to be eaten by animals; birds and humans. Their eating also ensures the safe and healthy life of the next generation of the tree or plant concerned.

In the case of most of the seeds and grains, part of it being destroyed is necessary for the healthy survival of the next generation. For example, if all the grains of wheat are allowed to grow as wheat, then there would be no space on the earth's surface for them to grow, much less for other trees and plants to grow. Eating the grains and seeds that are otherwise meant to be destroyed involves no hurting.

Food thus is available from various sources that require different degrees of hurting. At the lowest level there are items like tapioca, fruits, etc. that involve no hurting at all. At the topmost level is meat that entails cruel killing of animals. Essentially you must make a decision, where to draw the line beyond which you will not go.

It is sometimes argued that eating non-vegetarian food is essential to keep you healthy. Should this be so, elephants, completely vegetarian, would have been the weakest kind of animal in the world. On the contrary, the elephant is the biggest animal that is very strong also.

8

Some More Moral Instructions

ALL actions of all living beings basically are aimed at ensuring happiness. Every man being part of the total order, ensuring his happiness should not go against fellow humans as well as the total order of the world. How to exercise within reason one's own liberty is a problem that arises in this forementioned context. Many philosophers have formulated various principles to guide this tendency in us. The ethical principle that emerges from the pure philosophy we have developed in the earlier chapters would be this:

The action that ensures one's own happiness, while simultaneously ensuring happiness of all other beings, is ethically ideal. When one engages in selfish actions for one's happiness alone, without regard for others and the world, these actions are unethical. Such actions leave one spiritually impoverished, and leaves one in a self-created Hell. This ideal derives from the awareness that one Reality alone underlies the being of oneself and all else.

Moral instructions of various kinds are found scattered throughout the Indian scriptures. Some of these teachings relate how one's own actions have effect on the lives of others. Some other teachings are directly concerned with personal matters.

Fivefold Purities

A set of practices essential for your healthy life, enjoined in the Indian scriptures are known as *śuddhi-pañcaka* (fivefold purities). These are:

1. Bodily purity (*kāya-śuddhi*).
2. Purity of speech (*vāk-śuddhi*).
3. Mental purity (*manas-śuddhi*).
4. Purity of senses (*indriya-śuddhi*).
5. Purity of residence (*gṛha-śuddhi*).

1. *Kāya-śuddhi* consists of bathing daily in clean water, giving clearance to waste matter properly, keeping teeth and nails clean, ensuring cleanliness of the air one breathes and the food and water consumed, and keeping one's own limbs such as hands and feet clean.

2. *Vāk-śuddhi* is ensured by the following qualities of the words you utter: attractive pronunciation of syllables, their clarity, melodiousness of sound, aptness of words spoken, appealing harmony, not creating anxiety to others, being truthful, being receptive with proclivity towards self-learning, considering with noble heart what is favourable to all.

3. Your *manas-śuddhi* is ensured by the following qualities in you: straightforwardness, kindness, being friendly, gentleness, firmness, modesty, being angerless, engaged in meditation. (Straightforwardness implies your thoughts, words and actions becoming in harmony with one another.)

4. *Indriya-śuddhi* is achieved by your observing the following disciplines: not becoming involved in things not liked by you, neither torturing nor temptingly fondling the sense organs, not glorifying anything not praiseworthy.

5. *Gṛha-śuddhi* is ensured when you take care of the following: sunlight having ample access to the interior of the house, fresh air flowing across the rooms, discarding everything unhygienic, cleaning and sweeping the surroundings daily, not excreting in the vicinity of the house, burning incenses every morning and evening, letting its smoke spread everywhere in the house.

Five Great Sacrifices

As was seen earlier, our existence is as part of the total world order. A sense of responsibility is also in us as forming part of it. This sense of responsibility is used by us sometimes rightly and sometimes wrongly. When rightly used, it makes us accountable to its source, the total system of life. This responsibility transforms our lives into an offering of ourselves to the whole. This mental offering is poetically conceived of as a burnt sacrifice (*yajña*), a concept dear to almost all religions. Five such specific responsibilities are traditionally identified, and these five together are known as *pañca-mahā-yajñā*s (Five Great Sacrifices). These are:

1. Responsibility to the Absolute (*brahma-yajña*),

2. Responsibility to our ancestors (*pitṛ-yajña*),

3. Responsibility to natural phenomena, each conceived poetically as presided over by a deity (*deva-yajña*),

4. Responsibility to other living beings (*bhūta-yajña*),

5. Responsibility to the fellow humans (*manuṣya-yajña*).

1. Your responsibility to the Absolute or the one Ultimate Reality becomes fulfilled when you spend some time in contemplation each day, meditating on the "One Reality," and then spend some energy teaching this wisdom to others.

2. Begetting brilliant and worthy children, rearing them up properly, along with paying obeisance to the ancestors, fulfil your responsibility to ancestors.

3. Praying for the favours of natural phenomena (humans have no control over them) fulfil your responsibility to natural phenomena. It, in modern times, involves your responsibility to preserve the eco-system, for example, not burning plastic or polluting streams and rivers with garbage, sewage and industrial waste, not littering, etc.

4. Offering food and the like to animals and birds, etc. ensures your responsibility to other living beings having been fulfilled.

5. Adoringly doing service to guests, helping the sustenance of the dedicated full-time seekers of wisdom, helping those in trouble including your own helpers, fulfil your responsibility to fellow humans.

Instructions in the Taittirīya Upaniṣad

The *Taittirīya Upaniṣad* gives a long list of moral instructions to a disciple as he leaves the *gurukula* (the *guru*'s abode) for his home, after completing his formal education. This formality of taking leave, known as *samāvartana*, is equivalent to the graduation of modern times. All these are self-explanatory instructions.

1. Speak out the Truth and practise righteousness (*satyam vada, dharmam cara*).

2. Do not neglect continuing your self-learning (*svādhyāyān mā pramadaḥ*). This means, education does not end with.

3. After having brought to the Master wealth pleasing to him, do not cut off the line of progeny (*ācāryāya priyam dhanam āhṛtya prajātantum mā vyavacchetsīḥ*). (On

leaving the *gurukula*, the master is to be offered pleasing wealth to repay for all that he had taught, and then, on reaching home, should get married in order to ensure the continuity of progeny. See *pitṛ-yajña* stated above.)

4. Let there be no neglect of Truth (*satyāt na pramaditavyam*).

5. Let there be no neglect of righteouesness (*dharmāt na pramaditavyam*).

6. Let there be no neglect of happy life (*kuśalāt na pramaditavyam*).

7. Let there be no neglect of prosperity (*bhūtyai na pramaditavyam*).

8. Let there be no neglect of self-study and teaching (*svādhyāya-pravacanābhyām na pramaditavyam*).

9. Let there be no neglect of your responsibilities to nature (gods) and ancestors (*deva-pitṛ-kāryābhyām na prama-ditavyam*).

10. Be one to whom mother is a god (*mātṛ devo bhava*).

11. Be one to whom father is a god (*pitṛ devo bhava*).

12. Be one to whom master is a god (*ācārya devo bhava*).

13. Be one to whom guest is a god (*atithi devo bhava*).

14. Whatever deeds are blameless, they should be pursued, not others.

15. Whatever good practices are of ours they are to be followed by you, not others. (The master asks his disciple not to do everything he does, thinking of all such deeds are all ideal, but only those deeds that really are ideal.)

16. Knowledgeable persons superior to you are to be offered seats and comforted.

or

Nearby the seat wherein a knowledgeable person superior to you sits, you should not even breathe freely.

17. Gifts should be offered in plenty.

18. Gifts should be offered with modesty.

19. Gifts should be offered with awe.

20. Gifts should be offered with understanding.

21. Now if there is any doubt in you regarding any deed, any doubt regarding conduct, you should behave on such occasions as the knowers of Reality do, who may happen to be available, and who are unitively balanced, who need no direction from others, who are not harsh, and who love righteousness.

The Three *da*'s

The *Bṛhadāraṇyaka Upaniṣad* upholds three noble habits as of high value in human life. Poetically represented as three *da*'s, these three are *dāna* (offering gifts), *dama* (self-restraint) and *dayā* (kindness).

Offering gifts signifies your willingness to share with others what nature has brought to your possession. The value of the other two habits has been examined by us in the earlier sections.

The Ten Commandments

Supposedly revealed by God to the Prophet Moses are the well-known Ten Commandments, considered most valuable by the Jewish tradition. Of these Commandments, the first four are more of a religious nature, and the rest are of universal value. These are:

1. Honour your father and mother.

2. You shall not kill.

3. You shall not commit adultery.

4. You shall not steal.

5. You shall not bear false witness against your fellows.

6. You shall not covet anything that is your neighbour's.

The Two Commandments of Jesus

Jesus who continued the tradition of the Jews, later condensed these Ten Commandments into two. These two are:

1. You shall love the Lord, your God with all your heart, with all your soul, and with all your mind.

2. You shall love your neighbour as yourself.

— Mark, 12.30, 31

"The Lord your God" conceived both in Judaism and Christianity is equivalent to the one all-underlying Reality we have seen earlier. When you know that Reality, you perceive that Reality as the Substance of your own being, and loving God thus means loving the Reality in you. Then you realise also that the very same Substance constitutes all beings. You then realise yourself and others as of one Substance. Therefore you can see yourself in other beings. Then naturally the love you have for yourself is felt towards everyone else.

As is well known, this ideal of love is the highest moral value extolled in Christianity.

How to deal with our behaviour in relation to others, is one of the vexing moral problems faced by modern youth. Unacceptable behaviour towards others creates nuisance for oneself and others. Jesus gives us a clear directive to us in this respect. He says,

> Whatever you want men to do to you, do also to them.
> — Matthew, 7.12

Therefore let us ask ourselves when you are about to do something to another: "Does my action reflect how I would like to be treated by another?"

Honouring one's both parents as God-like has been seen by us acknowledged as a noble quality in the *Taittirīya Upaniṣad* we have already quoted. This view prevails in almost all the cultures of the world. Jesus for example, advises,

> Honour your father and your mother.
> — Matthew, 19.19

As a corollary to honouring one's parents, comes the habit of having respect for elders. They are to be honoured because the aged are more knowledgeable and more experienced in life. The Indian culture insists on treating all the elders as *guru*-like. Following them, rather than ridiculing them, is what is expected of those of the younger generation. Therefore it is taught in the Bible,

> You shall rise before the grey-haired and show respect to the aged.   — Leviticus, 19.32

Jesus again says,

> You shall not murder, you shall not commit adultery, you shall not steal, you shall not bear false witness.
> — Matthew, 19.8

Intolerance is one of the curses that torment the minds of modern youth, particularly in the light of the obsessions to make money at all costs. Before becoming intolerant, let us ask ourselves: does this intolerance give us troubles or peace of mind? If the former is the case, let us reflect on the situation. Tolerance brings us peace, intolerance brings trouble to oneself and to others. Jesus therefore asks us,

> To him who strikes you on the one cheek, offer the other also. Also from him who takes away your cloak, do not withhold your tunic either. — Luke, 6.29

We always judge the deeds, and words of others, and we feel doing so is easy. But more difficult is judging one's own actions and words. We forget or forgive our own wrongs, while we easily judge others harshly. Before judging others, let us judge ourselves; then we shall be able to look at others with a clearer and more compassionate vision. Jesus therefore gives this well-known advice:

> And why do you look at the speck in your brother's eye, but do not perceive the plank in your own eye? Or how can you say to your brother, "Brother, let me remove the speck that is in your eye," when you yourself do not see the plank that is in your own eye ? — Luke, 6.41, 42

Holy Quran

Quran (Koran), the basic scripture of Islam, abounds in direct instructions as to the way you should behave in your day-to-day life, in your personal affairs, social affairs and even political affairs. All such teachings have one basic principle underlying — the principle of brotherhood of man and the equality of humans before God.

Generally speaking, two kinds of actions are forbidden in Islam: One, the deeds that the society hates in the normal course and are harmful to oneself and others in general. Two, the deeds that one cannot reveal with a sense of honour to the members of one's own family and of the public, and the deeds one thinks are harmful to oneself if made public.

Likewise, the actions enjoined in the Koran are also of two types: One, all actions that do good to oneself and all else directly or indirectly, very soon or in the distant future. Two, the meritorious deeds performed keeping in mind the good of the human race in general, over and above their personal benefits. This latter kind of deeds generally would be of the same nature all through the world and at all times.

Absolutely speaking, the goodness or badness of a deed depends on the motivation behind it, not simply on the end-result. It would be different, if the satisfaction felt by a doer of actions, done with the understanding that all actions are simply part of the self-unfoldment of the one Absolute Reality, instead of being done by oneself for worldly personal gains.

Exploiting natural resources for the pleasure or convenience of the moment, or for financial gains, at the cost of irreparable destruction to nature, is totally unethical, is a hurt (*hiṁsā*) you inflict on nature and your descendants. The modern branch of study known as Ecology is based on this notion. Every human being should have the sense of responsibility to safeguard the eco-system, which ensures a healthy continuance of Nature and the sustainability of future generations.

There are many similar teachings available from non-religious sources also. What is important for us is not whether these teachings derive from religion or not, but whether these ennoble us or not.

Concluding this section, let us recall two most important teachings already mentioned: One, remain engaged in activities natural to your personal traits and that become inevitable as part of the overall flow of Nature. Perceiving such actions and their results, favourable or unfavourable, as taking place in the total Nature, keeps you liberated of sin or merit as related to those actions. In other words, do all your normal actions with a sense of complete detachment.

Two, be willing to treat both happiness and suffering in life with a sense of equanimity.

The most important point to be always aware of in this context, is that all these instructions are not simply meant to be learned to score high marks in your examination, but are to be practised in life everyday.

A glimpse across these moral instructions of various religions reveals how similar they are all. So is the core-content of the philosophical visions that underlie them also. That common core is nothing other than what we discussed in the first five chapters of this book.

9

The Goal of Life

WHAT is the meaning of this life? What should we attain in life? Why were we born at all? Such problems trouble most of the thinking people, particularly among the youth.

The emanation, existence and disappearance of all individual forms everywhere in all the worlds, as we have already seen, are part of the sportive self-manifestation of the one all-underlying Reality. The same Reality being what underlies our own being, our life also is to be perceived as part of the very same sportive self-manifestation of Reality. Everything related to life, both pleasurable and painful, will then be seen by each of us as part of a sport. Sports are meant to be enjoyed, never to be lamented on. Such a perception thus transforms life into a never ending flow of sportfulness. Even the painful old age and final death, the remerging of individual forms into the one Reality, also forms part of it.

Happiness

Securing a lucrative job is the most dominating aspiration of all the youth of the modern age. Why this craving for such a job? A job brings in enough money to support you. Does money meet your needs directly? No, money only buys all our needs, and meeting our needs makes us happy. Do you need money then for money's sake or for the sake of happiness? The latter is the case. That means, money as such does not make you happy. Not only money, but everything money can buy also does not make you happy; they are desired for the sake of happiness. Thus, happiness is the one goal of all of us.

Now, what is happiness? Happiness could be defined as "what we seek for the sake of its own." All else we wish to have is for the sake of happiness; happiness alone is what we yearn to have for its own sake.

Happiness could be seen as having two facets. One, negative in nature, represents the avoidance of sufferings. The other, of positive nature, is that of attaining felicity. The real happiness is where these facets meet.

Everything you come across, everything you perceive with your senses, everything you think of, is either liked by you, disliked by you, or you remain indifferent towards it. That means, everything you happen to know affects you in terms of its value for you, or the nature of happiness or suffering it arouses in you.

Suppose you feel happy when you possess something. Does that feeling of happiness originate from the object concerned, or does it well up from within you? When asking yourself, you find that the feeling arises from within you, and that the external object is merely instrumental in its arising.

Where was this happiness hiding in you unknown even to you? It should be nowhere else than in the Substance of your being. This Substance, as we know, is pure Consciousness in essence. Consciousness knows; Consciousness feels also. All the feelings imply pleasure or pain. In short, the Substance in your being and the experience of happiness are inseparable; the two really are one. You thus are happiness in essence; as you are pure Consciousness in essence. This Consciousness-content of yours always exists; it never arises, it never disappears. The real Happiness, thus, is always within you. This Happiness-content of your being is what assesses everything you happen to know as pleasurable, painful or neutral.

Happiness, admittedly, makes life meaningful. Then realising that Happiness unceasingly exists in you ensures unceasing happiness in life.

The awareness that the real Happiness is within you, as we have seen earlier, encourages you to keep the control of yourself, pure Happiness in essence, and not to be under the control of the potentially distracting pleasurable objects. Pure Happiness within you is everlasting, whereas the pleasurable objects and the pleasure they give are transitory. When we become aware of the value of these two happinesses, one naturally chooses the eternal.

Does this mean that the natural functions of the senses that form part of our being should be suppressed forcibly? No. To be in contact with their respective objects is natural to the senses. So with the other faculties also, i.e. mind, memory, ego, etc. Feeling pleasure, pain or indifference is also part of that natural function. When this happens in you, you can think of it as the Consciousness-content of your being finding expression as sense perceptions and all other knowledges; and the Happiness-content of your being as feelings of pleasure and pain. This attitude, when stabilised, helps you to be a detached witness to all natural functions of the senses and mental faculties. This sense of detachment keeps you free from the world and its temptations, while living as part of it.

Freedom

The trend of modern times is to count mere political and economic freedom as constituting actual freedom in life. This happens because of the dominance of political and economic interests of people and their struggle for these all over the world. But freedom is to be enjoyed in life at its various levels of interests.

What do you want to be free from? To be free from bondage. How do you become bound? When you find that, for the fulfilment of your interests, you have to depend on certain factors other than you, and consequently you identify yourself with those factors. For example, you find yourself one with your family, with a locality, with a caste, with a religion, with a nation, with a culture, with social organisations as well as with personal idiosyncrasies. It is the expectation of some kind of happiness that compels you to such identifications. This is the basic result of the illusion that your happiness derives from something external to you. This makes you bound to what you find yourself one with, and results in denying your nature-given freedom. This phenomenon has become so complicated and entangled in modern times that most of the people, born free though, are destined to perish bound from all angles.

Is it possible to free yourself from this snare? Yes, it is. Realise the cause of this bondage you are in. Your idea that your happiness depends on something else is the cause of all bondage. Were we not born free and alone? Are we not to die alone? Then it is better to live alone as well. To attain this aloneness, you do not have to run away from the world and everyone in it. Even when being in the middle of crowds, realise that you exist alone, and that your real happiness depends solely on you.

This self-reliant freedom is gained when you realise that the happiness you are in search of exists already in you, as your own essential content, which is pure Consciousness in essence. In short, becoming enlightened of what and who you really are, ensures your freedom that could also be called Liberation. This is the reason why the ancient seers repeatedly proclaimed, "Knowing yourself sets you free."

Now, how to actualise this Liberation in our day-to-day life?

First realise your oneness with the whole. Then, be aware that what underlies your being and that of the world is one Reality alone, which is pure Consciousness and Happiness in essence. Now understand that you are one of the countless fleeting forms in which this one Reality finds self-expression, happening because of the infinite creative urge inherent in Itself. Of these manifest forms, each is unique in intrinsic character; thus, you are also a unique person. Find out through self-examination what inherent qualities, traits, potentials and life interests make your personality unique. Now find out a vocation that fully fits with your personality. Do not forget that all these take place as part of the whole. Be also aware of the reality that the activities you are engaged in thus, really take place in Nature, that you are merely instrumental in relation to those actions. This awareness keeps you liberated of all actions. In other words, your self-knowledge is the firm basis that liberates you from all action-related bondages and sufferings, as well as from the senses of sin and merit and sense of identities. All these together make you fully liberated while being in this world.

Immortality

No one really likes death, especially when a youth. Even some of the aged fear death. All therefore try to avoid death at any cost. All this is despite the fact that death is inevitable. The opposite of death is immortality, and attaining it is always aspired by all. People, in the ordinary course, actualise this goal biologically by begetting offspring. They experience their continued existence through their children. A philosophical way of attaining immortality also exists.

Already seen is the fact that birth means the emerging of a new apparent form in the ever-existing Reality, and death, its re-merging into the same Reality. Before the emanation of the particular form, during the existence of the form, and after its dissolution, what really exists is one Reality alone. Before the emerging of a wave, during the existence of the wave and after its merging back into the ocean, what exists is water alone. This water was never born; it never dies; it is immortal. Likewise, even when living as an individual person destined to disappear, I really am the one birthless and deathless Reality, Consciousness and Happiness in essence. Realising this reality by properly knowing myself, makes me immortal when living here and now. Then the phenomena of birth and death become of no concern for me, for my identity is always with the immortal Reality. This is the philosophical way of attaining immortality.

The three values we have discussed here — Happiness, Liberation, Immortality — when closely examined, would be found to be not three experientially. Put otherwise, the highest Happiness, when experienced in actual life, would be felt to be the experience of liberation from all bondages, and from birth and death as well. So with the other two values also. Attaining the experience in which these three values become one is the highest goal attainable in human life.

10

Religion and Prayer

ONE of the peculiar features of modern civilised society is that, in a sense, everyone, unknowingly is religious. This will become clear later. This identity regarding religion is in one by birth even if one does not belong to any particular institutionalised religion, or even if one is against being religious. But to claim that such a feature is nature-born is also impossible, for all the existing religions are man-made groupings. Why is such a disposition part of human life?

The human peculiarity of having a religious identity is to be understood as related to the human nature of being a thinking animal. This thinking animal alone seems to have a religion. The thinking habit of man makes him dwell on the meaning of his own life. He thus formulates a notion regarding what should be his goal in life, conceived in a right way or wrong way. Then he strives to achieve it.

Associated with this characteristic is the one that differentiates human life from the life of all other animals — that all other animals simply live, but man leads his life. Where does he lead his life to? Towards the goal he has chosen. Everyone is free to choose this goal.

A goal is achieved always through some means. That is to say, an effort on the part of man is needed to achieve his goal that is freely chosen. This means also is freely chosen by him. Denying his freedom to choose his goal in life and not freely choosing the means to achieve it, render life meaningless. In short, absolute freedom with regard to choosing both ends and means of life, is what makes it meaningful for man. No one asks why it is so; it is something so fundamental in human nature.

This is only one side of the picture. Yet another side of life also exists. As we have explored earlier, our existence is a part of Nature's existence. The progression of our lives is also a part of Nature's flow. Achieving our chosen goal in life has to manifest through Nature's unfoldment of events. We have absolutely no control over these events. We must simply surrender our lives to flow in harmony with the flow of Nature. Man finds himself on the planet Earth as having no freedom of choice at all; his life is totally dependent on Nature.

Therefore, man finds himself caught between two opposite poles — the sense of freedom that makes life meaningful and his total dependence on Nature. To bring about an accord between these two extremes becomes a necessity for human happiness. An example of this necessity is observed when one well-wishing human being addresses another, enquiring, "Hello, how are you?" In this question one has a curiosity to know if one's efforts achieved the goal of life, in accord with Nature's flow of events.

Now how do you achieve this accord in our actual lives? To do this effectively one has to either bring down Nature's will and the chance elements of Nature to agree with the human will, or raise the human will up towards Nature's will, to live in harmony with it, or else both have to be brought to a middle point to coalesce. As we know, we have no control at all over Nature's will, we have control only on our own. Then the first choice would not work. Even bringing Nature's will half way down to meet the human will is also then not possible. The only choice then left is of human will being raised to agree with the unknown will of Nature. We can have full control over our own will. By re-channelling it, we can live in full accord with the flow of Nature. The chance element that controls Nature's flow, in Sanskrit, is termed *daivam*, and what is related to human effort, *pauruṣam*. Then the final fulfilment of the meaning of life is mentioned repeatedly in the epic *Mahābhārata* as resulting from the confluence of *daivam* and *pauruṣam*.

It is in the gap felt in the context of this exigency that religions step in to help man. The necessity of filling this gap is felt not only by believers but by non-believers also. Religions generally teach man the secret concerning the one ultimate Reality or God, and also how one can live in conformity with that Reality or as willed by God, by regulating his intentional activities. Religions, though being such, have taken divergent routes for the accomplishment of this purpose.

Now, how to have an understanding of the will of Nature or God? Religions, in the matter of finding a solution to this elusive problem, could generally be classified as prophetic religions and non-prophetic religions. The former are the ones like Judaism, Christianity and Islam. These religions originated from the teachings of certain prophets, the messengers of God (what we mean by "God" we have already seen). God (the one ultimate Reality) revealed to them the Truth concerning Him, and the way man should live in this world in accordance with the will of God. This revelation enables them to teach people what the Truth is, and encourage them to obey God's commandments, which pleases God. The responsibility of man, then, is to follow strictly such commandments while living in this world. Thus he finds a way to harmonise his life with the flow of Nature or will of God.

The non-prophetic religions like Hinduism, Buddhism, Jainism, Taoism, and Shintoism, all originated from the wisdom taught by certain enlightened masters and seers, many of them unknown. The only exception in this respect is Buddha. Though his life-story is well known, he is never treated as a prophet, nor has he claimed to be a messenger of God. On the other hand, he was "enlightened" which is the very meaning of the word "Buddha."

Slightly different from the way of the prophetic religions is that of the non-prophetic ones, in respect of helping man harmonise his will with Nature's. The former relies on the believing instinct of man, the latter relies on the thinking habit of man. These latter religions generally teach man to become aware of the one Reality that exists both in Nature and humans. Man realising his identity with the one Reality, enables him to transcend the duality between Nature and individuals, because both are manifest forms of one and the same Reality. The only difference is that Nature is the universal manifest form and man is an individual manifest form on both finding identity in the one Reality, bringing about an accord between the will of Nature and the will of man becomes of no relevance; it happens with no voluntary effort on the part of the man of wisdom.

Whether prophetic or not, all religions teach basically one and the same Truth. All the masters and prophets from whom religions originated, were the seers of that Truth — the Reality concerning life and its goal. The world being one, the phenomenon of life in it being one, its goal being one, what they visualised and what they taught are basically one. The differences would be only with respect to the languages in which they taught, the idioms and parables they used, the historical and cultural backgrounds that have influenced the way the teachings are presented, and to whom they are addressed. All such factors are merely incidental. Therefore it becomes transparent that the core content of the teachings from all the masters, seers and prophets is one and the same. All these teachings are aimed at the human race as a whole, and not to any particular section of it. The one common goal of all religions is but one alone — the betterment of human life, the happiness of man. Happiness in life is the one goal all religions encourage their followers to attain. This happiness is actualised by harmonising the will of man with the will of the Total Reality, called either God or Nature.

The prevailing hostilities among religions were not perpetrated by the seers or prophets. All of them stood for love between man and man. It really is a pity that religions that teach man to love each other, hate one another themselves. Fighting among religions does not enable one religion to win over another, because this fight is not between good and evil, but between good and good. All religions in themselves are good. Religions cannot be destroyed by fighting one another; it is the individuals that fight who alone perish.

This understanding pulls us back from religious rivalries, and prompts us to understand and appreciate the common core teaching in all religions. This ensures our living peacefully in the world as human beings who are willing to attune themselves with the whole, while being the unique individuals that they are.

Just as one can live as a free and happy individual with no hatred towards the followers of other religions, one can also live as a world-citizen while being the citizen of a particular nation, which has become an inevitable part of modern life.

Attuning an individual's life to the flow of Nature is to be acknowledged as a necessity in human life, even by those who do not believe in any religion or God. Admitting this necessity as forming the essential teaching of all religions it could well be said, non-believers and atheists also are religious in their own way. They also conceive and even teach certain ways by which the above-said end could be attained.

For example, Marxists who do not believe in God or religion. They think an individual can attain happiness in life through identifying oneself with society represented by state. In their perception society or state represents the total nature. Theirs also is a "belief." Atheists, likewise, "believe" that simply relying on one's reasoning power makes man happy. This reasoning faculty is a universal human phenomenon. This stand of atheists is also simply a "belief" never proved logically. Such beliefs have no more scientific validity than the belief that identifying oneself with God makes one happy. People, by believing in all such ideas or ideologies, aim ultimately at attaining happiness to its maximum.

Religion thus occupies an important place in human life, whether being so is acknowledged by man or not.

Prayer

Prayer is an essential practice observed by all religions. Even non-believers make some sort of prayer though not addressed to God. Their prayers, sometimes verbal and at other times silent, assume the form of wishing the best. Who is supposed to fulfil this wish? Only some unknown factor that can be nothing other than Nature. All prayer thus implies that it is God or Nature that ultimately controls everything in life. Yet the fulfilment of personal favours appears to be the goal of most of those who pray. The implication of such prayers is that, man decides what should happen in life, and the responsibility of working it out is of God. On the other hand, on admitting that everything happens as willed by God or Nature, what man can pray for would be this: "O Dear God (Nature), Thy will be done. May I become wise enough to make myself abide by Thy will."

If the supplicant is a small "I," the one prayed to is the biggest "I," the cosmic "I." A principled prayer should not be for any personal favour, but should be for the small "I" to become attuned and identified with the highest "I." If a favour is prayed for it should be aimed at the happiness of all.

People primarily exhibit one of the two types or bents of mind. The one is religious, emphasising sentiments and willing to believe. The other is scientific, emphasising reason. When it comes to the attainment of ultimate happiness, the great luminaries of both religion and science have historically come to remarkably similar conclusions. It is in this spirit of universality that I wish to conclude these reflections with two statements — one in the form of a prayer freely rendered from a work of Narayana Guru, and the second a direct quotation of Albert Einstein.

For those whose minds are inclined towards treating the one Consciousness-Reality as God, I offer the following prayer.

O God, protect us all here,
Lost in becoming's ocean.
You truly are the ship's captain
Who benignly helps us cross it safely.

Your footsteps, the mighty ship.
As everything, once well known,
Disappears in our minds,
May our minds also become
Merged in the Mind that you are.
O God, you are the creator;
You are every bit of creation as well;
The act of creation indeed you are;
You are also the material of creation.
You are the magic-like mystery
That makes the endless world appear;
And you are the great magician too;
It is you too who makes us disillusioned,
Allowing us thus to merge with your own Being.
In the deep ocean of your glory
Let us all become merged,
There to dwell and dwell for ever
In felicity Supreme.

On the other hand, for those with scientific minds, who prefer not to have a prayer at all, allow me to offer the following non-religious statement of the great sage of science, Albert Einstein:

A human being is a part of the whole, called by us "Universe," a part limited in time and space. We now experience ourselves, our thoughts and feelings as something separated from the Rest . . . a kind of optical delusion of our Consciousness. This delusion is a prison for us.

Our task must be to free ourselves from this prison by widening our circle of compassion to embrace all living creatures and the whole of Nature in her beauty.

Index